DALE JARRETT

A Lifetime to Win

by
David Poole

SPORTS PUBLISHING INC.
www.SportsPublishingInc.com

©2000 Sports Publishing Inc.

Series editor: Mike Persinger
Production manager: Erin J. Sands
Cover design: Julie L. Denzer
Coordinating editor: Claudia Mitroi
Photo editor: Sandy Arneson
Photos: *The Charlotte Observer*

ISBN: 1-58382-057-4
Library of Congress Catalog Card Number: 00-100051

SPORTS PUBLISHING INC.
www.SportsPublishingInc.com

Printed in the United States.

CONTENTS

Acknowledgments

Covering NASCAR isn't a bad way to make a living, especially when you get to do it for *The Charlotte Observer*, which has for a generation given stock-car racing the kind of coverage other papers are just now understanding the sport deserves.

Credit for that begins with the man who preceded me in the job as *The Observer*'s racing writer, the legendary Tom Higgins. Over his years in that role, "Pappy" built great relationships with important people in the sport and with readers of the newspaper. I benefit from those relationships every day, and for that I am deeply grateful.

I also would like to thank Gary Schwab, executive sports editor of *The Observer*, and Mike Persinger, deputy sports editor and my boss and friend, for having the faith to let me try to follow Higgins in that job. Without them, I would never have had the opportunity to see Dale Jarrett win the 1999 championship with such style and class.

It takes a lot of people to make a race team work, and that's also true for a newspaper's sports pages. Without the men and women who work on *The Observer*'s sports design and copy desks who catch my mistakes and present my stories, I couldn't do this job. So I thank them, too.

The list of people to thank for this project begins with the subject itself. Dale Jarrett is a worthy champion and a good man. He makes time for reporters in his remarkably hectic schedule and is always willing to give a thoughtful, honest answer to a legitimate question. It's hard to express how much a reporter appreciates that.

Thanks, too, to team owner Robert Yates, crew chief Todd Parrott and the rest of the members of the championship team for their time and cooperation.

Special thanks to Danielle Humphrey, the hard-working public relations representative for Jarrett's team who's one of the best in the business and one of the nicest people in the garage, and to Dan Zacharias, who tirelessly provides pit notes for all of Ford's Winston Cup teams. Their bosses at Campbell and Company should give them both a really big raise.

Thanks, also, to everyone at NASCAR, especially Tim Sullivan; to Rob Goodman, Denny Darnell, Chad Willis and everyone at Sports Marketing Enterprises; to Len Thatcher and Michael Payne, whose Winston Cup Updates make life easier for those covering the sport; and to Sports Publishing Inc. for their work on this book.

Most of all, thanks to my terrific wife, Karen, without whom life would not be complete. It's wonderful to know that after the long, tiring weekends away covering a race, I get to come home to Katy and the kids, David and Emily, to remember what's really important in this world. I love you guys.

—David Poole

Dale talks with reporters and photographers at Martinsville Speedway. (Todd Sumlin./Charlotte Observer)

INTRODUCTION

Imagine how it feels to stand wide-awake inside a dream.

Dale Jarrett knows that feeling.

On Dec. 3, 1999, he stood center stage at the Waldorf-Astoria Hotel in New York City with his family surrounding him. The fancy Grand Ballroom of the historic midtown Manhattan hotel was packed for the annual awards banquet for NASCAR's top series, but not a single seat was occupied.

Instead, everyone in the grand hall was on their feet, giving the circuit's 1999 champion one more standing ovation. Confetti floated down on every corner of the room as the spotlights swirled.

Moments earlier, the East Harlem Boys' Choir had saluted Jarrett's performance with a stirring rendition of the song "I Believe I Can Fly." At that moment, Jarrett probably felt like he very well could.

One week after celebrating his 43rd birthday, Jarrett had just accepted a check for nearly $3 million for winning the points championship.

"I don't know that I ever allowed myself to dream enough to think about winning a championship," Jarrett said. "I dreamed about winning races, but never to the point where I would dream about a championship.

"I would have had a better chance of jumping off the Empire State Building and living than winning the championship. It truly was the furthest thing from my mind."

It's funny how things work out sometimes.

Jarrett did go to the top of the Empire State Building during a whirlwind week in New York leading up to the banquet. He rang the bell to close a trading day at the New York Stock Exchange; had his picture taken with his car in Times Square; appeared on television and radio talk shows, and rode through Manhattan traffic in a limousine with a police escort clearing the way.

During the year, Jarrett got a jersey from members of an NBA team; threw out the first pitch at a major league baseball game; met Tour de France bicycling champion Lance Armstrong, and played golf with the legendary Arnold Palmer.

Not bad for a guy who once considered racing mainly something that only got in the way of what he really wanted to be doing.

Dale sits in his car before practice prior to qualifying for the NAPA 500. (Todd Sumlin/Charlotte Observer)

CHAPTER ONE

Lights Go Out on Broadway

Racing was always part of Dale Jarrett's life.

His father, Ned, won NASCAR's championship in 1961 and 1965 and remains one of the most respected men in the sport through his work as a television announcer.

As a young boy, Dale and his famous father often rode the track together for a race weekend. While Ned was racing against Richard Petty and David Pearson, Dale was in the infield playing with Kyle Petty and Larry Pearson.

Ned retired from driving but stayed in the racing business. The family operated Hickory Motor Speedway, one of the hundreds of short tracks where the popularity that racing enjoys today first took root.

Running a race track was a job for the whole family, and through much of his youth Dale wasn't particularly fond of his part of those chores. One of Dale's jobs was cutting grass, and at one point he convinced his father to buy a goat to help in that task.

"I wanted the goat to eat the grass off the side of a hill, thinking it would help me have more time to do what I wanted to do," Dale remembers. "All they did was eat the vinyl roofs and the interiors out of the old cars we had sitting out in a fenced-in area."

Ned laughs at the memory. "That goat ate everything but grass," he said.

Racing as a career?

Dale Jarrett didn't think much of that idea.

"I can assure you that when I was in the 10th or 11th grade, I couldn't have cared less", he said. "I would go to the races because I worked at the track during the summer. I really didn't care about racing."

Dale was born on Nov. 26, 1956, in the small town of Newton, N.C. Aside from spending many weekends at the race track with his famous father, his childhood was remarkably typical. He played all kinds of sports and soon found out that he was very good at many of them.

Jarrett made all-conference teams in football and basketball at Newton-Conover High School. But it was on the golf course where he showed the most talent. Dale loved golf. He even loved the practice that helped make him better. He spent as much time as he could at the course—when the race track's

Dale stands beside his car before a race. (Todd Sumlin/
Charlotte Observer)

grass didn't get in the way.

"I had a set of golf clubs," he said. "It didn't take anybody else for me to get to the golf course to practice and play. I could ride my bike to baseball practice. They'd get me to school and we had football practice right after that. It wasn't a big deal to play these other sports. It didn't seem to inconvenience anybody.

"I could see how difficult it was to get involved in racing. I kept asking people to give me a chance. They would tell me to get some experience and come back and see them. These were people I had known a long time. It was kind of hard to get the experience when they wouldn't give me the chance."

He finally got a chance in 1977.

Andy Petree and Jimmy Newsome, who both had attended the same high school Dale did, were building a Chevrolet Nova to race. They needed an engine, though, and didn't have the $2,500 or so it would cost to get one to power their car around the track.

Dale had an idea. He turned to his father to help raise money to buy the race engine. The deal was that Dale would get to drive the car with that engine under its hood.

So, in April, Jarrett entered his first race at Hickory. Jarrett had practiced by himself on the track, but until that night he had never been on a track with other cars. The car wasn't ready on race day in time for any practice or for qualifying, either.

Jarrett, a rookie in every sense of that word, started last in his first race.

Inside that car, Jarrett was quickly learning that there was a lot more to racing than grass-eating goats. He never knew what fun he had been missing.

"It was just unbelievable," he said. "I mean, I had no idea. I literally ran from down on the track upstairs and told my mom and dad, 'I found it! This is what I want to do!'"

Jarrett finished ninth in that first 25-lap race.

"I made $35," Dale said, "and I still have the pay envelope."

Dale takes the checkered flag to complete his qualifying run for the NAPA 500. (Todd Sumlin/Charlotte Observer)

CHAPTER TWO

A Long Road

Success was never an overnight thing for Dale Jarrett in a race car.

It took him until 1980 to get his first victory in a race at Hickory, but Jarrett pressed on. Eventually, he worked his way into NASCAR's Grand National series.

Today, Grand National series races are run at many of the sport's largest tracks and draw crowds of up to 100,000. At its beginning, however, the series provided racing for many of the smaller, shorter tracks left behind when NASCAR's top series was reshaped to concentrate on bigger tracks.

In 1982, the first year in the history of the series, Jarrett drove 29 races and had just one top-five finish. He won four poles the next season and finished in the top five 17 times. In his first four seasons in Grand National racing, Jarrett ran 120 races and finished 10th or better in 72 of them. But he still could not find a way to get a win.

Finally, in 1986, his first victory came in a Pontiac in a race at Orange County Speedway in Rougemont, N.C. It was a track not too different from the Hickory track where he learned how to race—a lap at Orange County covered .375 miles; Hickory was a .363-mile track.

It had taken him 142 starts to win a race. He would win, fittingly, at Hickory the following year. In 1988, he got his first "big track" win, at Charlotte Motor Speedway in May. He won again at Charlotte and at Darlington in 1990.

Even after he moved up into the Winston Cup circuit, Jarrett continued to compete in Grand National races. He has, in fact, competed in at least one Grand National race in every year since the series began in 1982.

In 324 career Grand National races, Jarrett has 11 victories and 170 top-10 finishes. He has won $1,477,592 in that division.

"My story isn't a lot different from a lot of other people," Jarrett said of his years in the Grand National series. "We raced on just what little money we could get. I guess people assumed a lot of times that because I was Ned Jarrett's son that we had plenty of money and didn't have to worry about that, but that certainly wasn't the case."

He got his first chance to drive in a Winston Cup race on April 29, 1984, at Martinsville, Va. He started 24th and finished 14th.

He raced in two more Winston Cup races that

Dale climbs into his car prior to qualifying for the NAPA 500. (Todd Sumlin/Charlotte Observer)

year and one more in 1986. Jarrett finally got the chance to run for rookie of the year in 1987, running 24 races for car owner Mike Freedlander. He managed two top 10s, but fell out early in 11 of the races and won just $143,405 in a season during which Davey Allison had one of the greatest rookie years in NASCAR history.

Over the next decade, the coincidence of Allison—the son of NASCAR legend Bobby Allison—and Jarrett being rookies in the same season would come to take on great irony.

Ned Jarrett (left) looks on as his son snacks on corn chips in the team hauler. (Todd Sumlin/Charlotte Observer)

CHAPTER THREE

Starting the Climb

J arrett had a son, Jason, from his first marriage. He and his second wife, Kelley, had their first child together in 1988—Natalee was born on March 26—during a season in which Dale was trying to establish himself on NASCAR's top circuit.

He was in a Cale Yarborough-owned car for 19 races—the 19 in which Yarborough didn't race in what would be the three-time champion's final season as a driver.

Jarrett was scheduled to drive the season's other 10 races for Hoss Ellington, but that deal didn't last the season. Jarrett wound up driving one race for Ralph Ball and another in a car owned by Buddy Arrington.

It was another tough year—Jarrett managed only one top-10 finish and was out early in 14 of the 29 starts. But when Yarborough announced his retirement, he hired Jarrett to drive for him in 1989 season.

Jarrett got his first two top-five finishes that season, but he also failed to finish 11 races. Toward the end of that season Yarborough announced he had hired Dick Trickle to replace Jarrett in 1990.

So, at the beginning of a decade that would end with him reigning as the sport's champion, Jarrett did not have a Winston Cup ride. That changed just a few days before the birth on April 11, 1990, of Dale and Kelley's second daughter, Karsyn.

Neil Bonnett, after being involved in a 13-car wreck during a race at Darlington, S.C., was suffering from amnesia. The Wood Brothers, one of the most respected teams in NASCAR history, needed a driver to take over as Bonnett recovered. Jarrett got the call.

It started out as a one-race deal for the next event at Bristol, on April 8, but turned into a two-year stay that helped turn Jarrett's career around. Jarrett ran 24 races for the Woods in 1990, finishing fourth at Atlanta for the best of his seven top-10 finishes.

The following year, on Aug. 18, 1991, Jarrett would finally see a dream come true.

The race was the Champion 400 at Michigan Speedway. Davey Allison, driving a car owned by Robert Yates, found himself racing during the final two laps side-by-side with Jarrett in the No. 21 Ford.

Door-to-door they raced, two sons of former

Dale moves into turn one while qualifying for the NAPA 500.
(Todd Sumlin/Charlotte Observer)

NASCAR champions whose paths had crossed as rookies in 1987 but then headed off in different directions. While Jarrett struggled for a foothold on the sport's top level, Allison was emerging as a star. Allison had finished second to his father, Bobby, in the 1988 Daytona 500 and had earned his 11th career Cup victory earlier in 1991 in the season's first race at the Michigan track.

On that August afternoon, however, the nose of Jarrett's Ford reached the finish line less than one foot—after 400 miles of racing—ahead of Allison's in one of the most thrilling finishes in NASCAR history!

For the Wood Brothers, it was victory No. 95 but the first since 1987. For Jarrett, the win in his 129th career Cup race was a first step toward his destiny.

Dale talks with his crew chief during testing at Lowe's Motor Speedway. (Christopher A. Record/Charlotte Observer)

CHAPTER FOUR

Coming of Age

In the days before his first career victory at Michigan, Jarrett wrestled with a decision that would eventually mark the beginning of his rise to stardom.

Joe Gibbs, the Super Bowl-winning coach of the NFL's Washington Redskins, was starting his own NASCAR team. On the Tuesday before Jarrett won at Michigan, Gibbs announced Jarrett would be his driver beginning with the 1992 season.

Jarrett's decision to leave the Wood Brothers was a tough one.

"It was more than me being a driver for them," he said. "They made me feel like a part of their family. It's a deal I would have never left if it wasn't for so many other business opportunities I am going into."

Jarrett's crew chief at the new team, for which he would drive Chevrolets carrying the No. 18, would be Jimmy Makar. Makar is married to Jarrett's sister, making them brothers-in-law.

The brand new team finished second at Bristol and third at the July race at Daytona to highlight eight top-10s in their first season, laying a solid foundation for Jarrett's first real taste of being among the best in racing.

The Daytona 500 is NASCAR's most important race. It opens each year's schedule and teams spend their entire off-season getting ready to compete at the 2.5-mile high-banked oval in Daytona Beach, Fla.

For the first time in his Winston Cup career, Jarrett earned a front-row starting position for the 1993 Daytona 500. He lined up outside of Kyle Petty to start the race on Valentine's Day.

High above the track, sitting in the CBS television broadcasting booth, Ned Jarrett watched as his son drove the No. 18 car into contention. Years before, when he was 7, Dale had watched from the infield as Ned ran out of gas while leading on the last lap of the same race. Ned didn't win that day or any other day at Daytona during his driving career.

With less than two laps to go, Dale Earnhardt had the lead with rookie Jeff Gordon riding on his rear bumper. Jarrett had his Chevrolet running higher up on the track, and when Earnhardt bobbled just a little Jarrett got alongside the race leader.

Geoffrey Bodine, in a Ford, lined up behind Jarrett's car and gave Jarrett a boost because of the way the air affects way cars at Daytona. Jarrett inched forward and found himself leading the Daytona 500 with less than a lap to go.

As Dale tried to hold off Earnhardt, one of the sport's greatest drivers, as they raced back toward the checkered flag, Ned's CBS colleagues backed out of the broadcast and let the race leader's father call the action. Ned coached Dale through the final corners, and when it became clear that Earnhardt wasn't going to catch him, Ned got to tell America that "Dale Jarrett is going to win the Daytona 500!"

Jarrett had won the biggest race there is!

"I realized, of course, that the Daytona 500 was the biggest show in NASCAR racing," he said.

"But I doubt any driver really realizes how big it is and how much interest it attracts until he wins it."

Jarrett didn't win another race in 1993, but he finished in the top five 12 more times and wound up fourth in that season's points race—by far the best finish of his career. His winnings for the year were $1,242,394; nearly three times as much as he'd ever won in any previous year in Winston Cup.

It seemed that the Joe Gibbs Racing team might be on its way toward racing for a championship in 1994. But things don't always work out that easily. Jarrett's road to the top still had some detours ahead.

Dale sits in his car and prepares for the next race.
(Todd Sumlin/Charlotte Observer)

The Path Not Taken

Jarrett would get his third career victory at Charlotte Motor Speedway in October of 1994, but that would turn out to be a disappointing year.

Instead of improving on the success of 1993, the Joe Gibbs Racing team seemed to take a step backward. The No. 18 car managed only nine top-10 finishes, half as many as the year before, and Jarrett wound up 19th in the points standings. Critics began to surface, questioning whether he was good enough to lead a top-level team.

The problems Jarrett's team was facing, however, were nothing like what had befallen Robert Yates Racing, the team for which Davey Allison had been driving when Jarrett edged him for Jarrett's first win at Michigan in 1991.

In 1993, Allison had been killed when a helicopter he was flying crashed as he tried to land it at the Talladega, Ala., race track. Ernie Irvan had taken over as Yates' driver in the No. 28 Ford, but in August of 1994 Irvan had been critically injured in a crash during a practice session at Michigan.

Irvan had defied the odds by merely surviving the crash, and would eventually make a miraculous recovery to return to driving. That was going to take time, however, and Yates needed a driver for the 1995 season.

Kelley Jarrett had been pregnant with her first child when Dale went to drive for Cale Yarborough in 1988, and was about to deliver her second when Dale got the call from the Wood Brothers in 1990. Perhaps it was an omen that, as the 1994 season approached its end, she was expecting another baby. Zachary would be born on Dec. 8, 1994—and the Jarretts faced another crossroads in their lives.

Dale had decided he would leave Gibbs' operation to form his own race team. When Yates asked him to drive the No. 28 Ford until Irvan was able to return, Jarrett decided to take that opportunity for 1995.

"That was a very, very difficult decision and probably the hardest one," Jarrett said. "But I felt I was being led to Robert Yates Racing for a reason."

Jarrett still thanks Gibbs for giving him the opportunity to drive his race cars. Jarrett also credits Gibbs, a devout Christian, for being a role model who helped Jarrett change the way he was living his life.

Robert Yates keeps an eye on his team as Dale prepares to take the track. (Todd Sumlin/Charlotte Observer)

By May of the 1995 season, however, nobody involved with the decision to put Jarrett in the No. 28 Ford was sure it had been the right decision. The team, which had been in the race for the championship when Irvan was hurt the previous season, wasn't off to a good start. Jarrett started first—his first career pole—for the season's first race at Daytona, but hadn't enjoyed much success after that. The same old questions about Jarrett's abilities surfaced one more time.

At Charlotte, Yates asked driver Hut Stricklin to drive the No. 28 for a few laps to see if he could make the car go any faster than Jarrett could. The team's key members held a long meeting the week before the Coca-Cola 600 on Memorial Day weekend to talk about their problems. Jarrett was offered a chance to resign, but elected to tough it out hoping things would not get so bad that Yates would fire him.

The pressure eased in July when Jarrett won a race at Pocono, Pa., but just a couple of weeks later Jarrett learned just how uncertain the future was.

"Robert (Yates), Kelley and myself were riding in a car in Indianapolis in the early part of August," Jarrett said. "Robert said, 'You know, I just don't think two teams would ever work for me. They can't make Victory Lane big enough for two teams and two cars, so somebody is always going to be disappointed and that's a difficult situation.'"

Jarrett knew the Irvan was on the way back. What Yates was saying was that when Irvan was ready to take over the No. 28 Ford, there wouldn't be a car for Jarrett to drive.

Jarrett went back to work looking for sponsorship for a team that he would own. He actually had a contract for enough money to go racing in 1996, but it was with a national restaurant chain that features waitresses wearing revealing outfits.

"It wouldn't have exactly fit the image that I was trying to portray," Jarrett said. "But at that time, I had to worry about my family and making a living and getting something started. I really thought that's what I wanted to do."

The still-unsigned contract was on his desk in mid-August when Jarrett left to go to Bristol for a race. That weekend, Yates told Jarrett he had changed his mind.

"I knew there was a reason I didn't sign the contract," Jarrett said. "Robert came to me in Bristol and offered me the opportunity, and I realized then and there that's why I hadn't signed that contract. There was going to be something there waiting for me. Everybody says God works in mysterious ways. You just don't know. Good things come to those to wait. There, I waited, and look what happened."

Irvan would return late in the 1995 season, then come back full-time in 1996 to take back the seat in the No. 28. Jarrett would head up a new team, driving the No. 88 Fords.

Looking back now, of course, it seems like it would have been an easy decision to make. But at the time, there were no guarantees.

"We heard all of the things, like that we were going to get Ernie's leftovers and second-rate stuff," Jarrett said. "I knew that's not the way Robert Yates would ever go about any business. If he's going to do something it's going to be done right. But even if it would have been the case, that's better than 80 percent of the things that are out here anyway."

Jarrett had learned a lot during his years of struggling to make it to the sport's top level. One of the most important things was about what it takes to build a winning team.

"This sport is so totally different than other sports," he said. "It requires money and a lot of people don't have that, so you have to work your way around that. I'm not saying your success is totally dependent on those dollars, but a lot of it is.

"It doesn't matter how good a race driver you are and the talent that you have. Until you surround yourself with the people who know how to use those talents, you're not going to be able to make it all happen."

And for Jarrett, it was all finally about to start happening.

Dale and Robert Yates pose for the cameras at Martinsville Speedway. (Todd Sumlin/Charlotte Observer)

Pieces for the Puzzle

If Todd Parrott had looked closely enough on his road to where he is today, he might have noticed Dale Jarrett's footprints. Their routes were remarkably similar.

Parrott's father, Buddy, is one of the most respected mechanics and pit crew chiefs in NASCAR history. Like Jarrett, Todd spent a great deal of his childhood following his dad to race tracks across the Southeast and the rest of the country where NASCAR traveled. He started working on cars as a teenager and eventually earned a spot on Rusty Wallace's crew, where Parrott was part of the championship team in 1989.

He was still working with Wallace's team in 1995 when Robert Yates called him to offer him a job as crew chief for the new team he was forming for Jarrett for 1996.

"Robert gave me a chance," Parrott said. "He called and asked me and said, 'Are you ready to do it?' And I said, 'Well, I don't know if I'm ready or not, but you're probably not ever going to call back again if I don't take this job.'"

Parrott served as Irvan's crew chief for the final two races of the 1995 season, but quickly went to work assembling a group for the new team. Never once, he says, did he doubt that the team would be a success.

"I have been with successful teams all my life," Parrott said. "Every place I had ever been as a mechanic we won races."

He saw no reason for that to change in his new job, either.

"I have a lot of confidence in what I do and in my abilities," Parrott said. "I had confidence in the guys I hired there to do the job. I had total confidence in what they did. I knew we had good cars. I had done everything at other race teams except have the crew chief title. I knew that we were going to be strong."

The new team could not have had a better start.

Jarrett opened the 1996 season by winning a season-opening special event race for drivers who had won poles in 1995. A week later, he came back and won the Daytona 500 for the second time in his career.

Parrott wasn't surprised.

"We worked really hard all winter long," Parrott said. "We knew when we rolled into

A crew member works on Dale's car during testing at Lowe's Motor Speedway. (Todd Sumlin/Charlotte Observer)

Daytona that we were going to be good. I knew that if I did my job and had everything just right, we could win the race."

With Parrott on his side, Jarrett had turned the corner.

They won the Coca-Cola 600 at Charlotte in May, then prevailed in a thrilling duel with Irvan, now his Robert Yates Racing teammate, to capture the Brickyard 400 at Indianapolis Motor Speedway. Nobody else has ever won the Daytona 500 and the Brickyard 400 in the same year. Jarrett then added a win at Michigan as he battled his way into the points race.

With two races left in the season, Jarrett was third, 76 behind leader Terry Labonte. Jarrett fell 99 points behind after finishing eighth at Phoenix, and wound up 89 behind Labonte and 42 behind Jeff Gordon after the last race at Atlanta.

Jarrett's winnings of $2,985,418 that year were

only part of the story. He won four times, finished second in seven more races and finished fifth or better 17 times in 31 races. As the 1997 season approached, Jarrett was ranked among the favorites to contend for a championship.

He didn't disappoint. Jarrett won seven races, five in the second half of the season as he charged into the thick of a three-way title fight with Gordon and Mark Martin.

The most impressive—and timely—of his victories came in the season's next-to-last race at Phoenix. Jarrett fell a lap down early in the race, but fought back to win going away. Gordon, who had led Martin by 125 points and Jarrett by 145 coming into the race, suffered a flat-tire late in the race and finished 17th. The teams went to the last race at Atlanta with Gordon leading Jarrett by 77 points and Martin by 87.

Gordon wrecked his car in practice on Saturday morning and had to use a backup Chevrolet in the race. He started 37th, knowing he had to finish 18th or better the win the title. Jarrett and Martin, meanwhile, battled among the leaders all day. Jarrett finished second to Bobby Labonte, with Martin third. Gordon, though, managed to get up to 17th place and won the championship by 14 points over Jarrett. Martin finished 29 behind.

Jarrett and his team were disappointed they didn't win the 1997 championship. But they had won seven races, finished in the top five 20 times and earned $3,240,542. It's a good sign when a team can be disappointed with results like that, because it means they're still hungry to reach the top.

Jarrett's team wouldn't get to reach that goal in 1998, however. Gordon dominated that season, winning 13 races and running away with the championship. Jarrett, however, did win at Darlington, Dover and Talladega—bringing his career total to

Dale is chased by autograph seeking fans and the media. (Todd Sumlin/Charlotte Observer)

18 victories. The Talladega win also brought $1 million bonus as part of a new program involving five of the season's most important races, and Jarrett cracked the $4 million mark in earnings for the first time in his career.

Dale and Robert Yates talk atop their team transporter at Martinsville Speedway. (Todd Sumlin/Charlotte Observer)

Putting it All Togeher

The most important thing that happened for Jarrett and Robert Yates Racing in 1998 came after the season was over.

"We sat down at the end of the year and said, 'Here are the things that we want to do. This is the procedure, the people that we want to bring into our organization,'" Jarrett said. "We didn't talk about doing these things to win races. We did it to win the championship. These were the things we needed to win the championship.

"That wasn't being cocky. That was what we had observed and gone through in the past three years in watching other people win championships and what we felt like cost us the opportunity to win a championship in that period of time.

"We set out to win the championship in 1999. That's what we intended on doing. If you don't go in with that mindset, truly thinking about that, then it makes it difficult to carry that out."

At the team's holiday party in 1998, Jarrett handed out cards to each person connected to the No. 88 Fords. "It's amazing what can be accomplished if no one cares who gets the credit," the card read.

Jarrett went to Daytona with high hopes for the season's first race. But that's when things literally got turned upside down.

On Lap 135 of the Daytona 500, Jarrett's Ford spun off Turn 4 after making contact with Kenny

Irwin, who had followed Irvan into the No. 28 car a season earlier. Jarrett and Irwin were running in a pack of 20 cars at the time of the spin, and the accident that followed damaged more than a dozen cars.

Jarrett's car turned a complete roll in midair before coming to rest on its wheels. Jarrett wasn't hurt, but the car was done for. He finished 37th in the season's first race.

"That certainly could have put us in a tail-spin," Jarrett said of his team. "But we realized we had prepared a good car. We had done exactly what we set out to do, which was to go to Daytona, be competitive and give ourselves a chance to win. We had done all of that up until the point the accident happened.

"The next thing we had to do was remember that over the winter we had prepared ourselves, we knew that there were going to be a couple of bad

The sun glimmers off Dale's Ford as he takes to the track. (Todd Sumlin/Charlotte Observer)

races throughout the season. You can't go through 34 races and not have some problems. We got one of them out of the way early. We had to make sure we were even better than what we anticipated we would have to be. We had to continue with the plan."

Jarrett ran second the next weekend at Rockingham. After finishing 11th in the season's third race at Las Vegas, he ran off six top-five finishes in the next seven races. When he got to Richmond for the race there on May 15, he was second in points, just 55 behind Jeff Burton.

Jarrett started 21st at Richmond, but patiently worked his way into position to challenge the leaders. On Lap 369, with just 32 laps remaining, he passed Martin and took the lead in the race. He went on for his first victory of the season and also took over the points lead.

It was a position he would come to be very familiar with.

Jarrett dominated the field to win three races later at Michigan, then squeezed out enough gas mileage to hold on for a win at Daytona on July 3. A month later, he joined Gordon as the only two-time winner in the six-year history of the Brickyard 400.

The victories were important—a champion driver wants to win every time he gets in the race car. But Jarrett knows that it's just not possible to do that.

The system used to determine NASCAR's championship rewards consistency.

A driver gets a certain number of points based on his finishing position. The better his finish, the more points he gets. He also gets bonus points for leading at least one lap in a race, and the driver who leads the most laps in a race gets more bonus points.

The most points a driver can score in a race is 185—if he wins and leads the most laps. The driver who finishes 43rd, or last, gets 34 points. So the difference between first and last can be as much as 151 points per race. Good finishes help build the points total, but bad finishes can be disastrous.

Jarrett and his team dodged disaster masterfully. At California, for instance, Jarrett shredded a tire and later was penalized for coming down pit road while it was closed, but he still rallied to finish fifth. Days like that one that would help make the difference during the season.

As the summer wore on, Jarrett's consistency began to show up in the points race. In the 21 races after the problem at Daytona, Jarrett never finished worse than 11th. He finished worse than sixth only twice. After 22 races, Jarrett had a 314-point lead over Martin and had begun to think about what it would mean to win a championship.

"Are we meant to win a championship?" Jarrett said. "I don't know. We'll know here shortly. It may not be. And because of my belief in God I can fully accept what He throws at us here.

"If it's to learn to deal with not winning, we can do that. If it's to learn how to deal with winning, there's a lot of things we have to think about there, too, because there's more reasons than us being able to win a championship and collect millions of dollars. There are other things on our plate.

"In 1997, winning the number of races that we did and coming that close it gave us other opportunities and put us more in the limelight and spotlight. There are things you have to deal with there. There's a lot of really, really good things that come with that, but there is also the downside of it. There are a lot of negative things that go with popularity. I can assure you of that. You have to learn to deal with that. I think we have kind of been put through those tests here and now maybe we're ready."

Dale watches as his crew works on his car in the garage area during practice for Pole Night at Lowe's Motor Speedway. (David T. Foster/Charlotte Observer)

A Final Trial

Jarrett and his team rolled into Bristol Motor Speedway for the Goody's 500 on Aug. 28 in command of the points race. But Jarrett had a little problem in qualifying and started the race 25th, meaning he would have to make his pit stops on the backstretch at the short, treacherous Bristol track.

That qualifying misstep proved costly. Just 77 laps into the race, Jarrett spun. His car went across the track, then bounced back up into traffic. Jarrett's

Ford was one of several cars badly damaged. He managed to stay in the race, but couldn't keep up with the fast cars and wound up in another wreck less than 25 laps later.

Jarrett's crew had no magic to prevent disaster on this day. He finished 38th, his worst finish of the year, and saw his points lead over Martin shrink to 213.

The next weekend, Jarrett thought his Ford was good enough to win him his first pole of the season, for the Southern 500 at Darlington. He drove it just a little too hard into the final turn, however, and spun. That doomed him to a 36th-place starting spot and another backstretch pit stall. He finished 16th in the rain-shortened race and led Martin by just 168 points.

"We hadn't been living on the edge every week," Jarrett said. "That's something you can't do as a driver or as a crew chief. If you're on that edge every week in trying to do your job, then you're going find yourself getting in trouble.

"When I tried to get myself a little bit too much on the edge I got myself in trouble this year. In qualifying at Darlington and trying to be a little bit too much on the edge at Bristol in the race, so those were things that got us."

Jarrett hadn't forgotten the plan, though, and when he finished third in the next race at Richmond the momentum swung back his way. Martin had the problems this time; finishing 35th and falling out of second place in the points race. Bobby Labonte was now Jarrett's closest challenger, and he was 270 points behind.

Labonte would finish eighth or better in the season's final 10 races, closing it out with a win at Atlanta. But Jarrett had built too much of a cushion. Jarrett finished seventh or better in eight of those last 10 races. When he finished fifth at Home-

Dale talks with reporters and photographers. (Todd Sumlin/ Charlotte Observer)

stead-Miami Speedway in the 33rd race of the 34-race season, Jarrett clinched the championship.

When he parked the car on the frontstretch of the Florida track, Jarrett jumped out and pumped his fists triumphantly at the crowd. His crew was there to greet him. So was his family. His father, Ned, and mother, Martha, wiped tears from their eyes. His car owner, Robert Yates, was almost too stunned to speak.

Only once before in history had a father and son won NASCAR's top title—Lee and Richard Petty had both been champions. Ned and Dale Jarrett had now joined them.

The Atlanta race could have been nothing more than a victory lap for the No. 88 team. But that's not how champions race. Labonte won that day, but Jarrett passed Jeremy Mayfield in the final laps to take second. He was a battling to the end.

The final margin was 201 points.

Dale was getting excited at the real possibility of winning the championship. (Todd Sumlin/Charlotte Observer)

A Story to Inspire

Jarrett held the lead in the points race for the final six months of the 1999 season, giving him plenty of time to anticipate what it might be like to be the guest of honor when stock-car racing assembled in New York for its annual post-season awards banquet.

At the same time, he also had all of that time to worry about how disappointing it would be for him and for his race team if something happened to deny them the title.

"It is such a joy that it brings chills at times to think about it," Jarrett said at one point late in the season. "But on the other side of it, I know it could be gone as quickly as it appears to be that close.

"This definitely has to be the longest season there has ever been. It is more difficult than I ever anticipated being out front for this length of time trying to hold that lead. It seems to be the nature of people to look for you to fail. We certainly don't want it to happen, and if it happens would it be devastating? It would be difficult to handle. But it wouldn't be the end of the world. We want this really bad as a team.

"I only think about it when I am awake. Other than that, I can put it behind me."

As the weeks went by and his consistency kept the lead above the 200-point mark, the excitement grew.

Jarrett was on his way to a championship. Even

a flat tire that put him a lap down in the middle of the race at Phoenix, the 32nd of the season's 34 races, couldn't sidetrack him. As he and his team had done all year, Jarrett overcame that and finished sixth. When he drove a smart, smooth race the next weekend at Homestead-Miami, it was finally over.

"I am a believer in fate," Jarrett said. "I think there are certain times, whether you believe in it or not, there's a way that things are going to happen. Sometimes the more you try to make changes in that, the worse off you are.'"

"When we blew the tire at California, that happened going into Turn 1 inside of a car. How I missed him and them missed the wall, I don't know. It wasn't anything I did; I was just lucky to be holding on. But it happened for us. A lot of times those tires will stay on the rim, but mine came off and got on the middle of the race track where they had

Dale and Robert Yates pose for the cameras. (Todd Sumlin/
Charlotte Observer)

to throw a caution. That enabled me not to lose a lap and then I was able to make up the time."

Jarrett's week in New York was even more exciting than he dreamed it would be. The whole time he was enjoying it, he couldn't help but think about other drivers and race teams that work long hours trying to get their chance at winning a championship.

"I have heard a lot of people say, 'You deserve it,'" Jarrett said. "Maybe I do. But there are a lot of people who I can look around and say, 'Man, they certainly deserve it.' Especially now that I am fortunate to see just how special this is, I wish everybody could have one. I want to win more than one, but this is something all of the competitors should be able to enjoy."

Jarrett remembered how he had felt the past three years after finishing third, second and third in the points race.

"There's no more inspiration than sitting out in that audience and looking at that head table up there," he said. "You come back so ready to go and so pumped up.

"I get to enjoy more of the spoils than the rest of the guys. But we're going to enjoy it, and we're going to try to use it as a motivation, too. I think that sitting up there will be motivation for myself and the rest of the guys, to say, 'Hey, this is where we want to be. We've got to continue to work hard to get back there.'"

Jarrett also hopes his story of perseverance against all the obstacles he has had to face in his career can provide a lesson for others, too.

"I hope as much as anything that may come out of this championship is that it could be an in-spiration to others, whether they are looking to get into auto racing or any other sport or any kind of business," the champion said. "Take a look at where we have all been, what we came through and how we got here. Use that as an inspiration that if you set out to do something, you can make it happen with hard work and dedication."

Jarrett says that's a lesson that is understood when he talks with his own children and with other young people with whom he gets to visit as a NASCAR star.

"You can do and be anything you want to in this country," Jarrett said. "Nobody is stopping you from doing it. You work and work to accomplish something.

"You have, living in the United States of America, the opportunity to do whatever you want. It's out there. If it's playing sports or being a teacher or a doctor or a lawyer, whatever you want to do, you can do it. Don't let anybody tell you that you can't try to do that. You just have to find what is right for you."

Dale, who clinched the 1999 Winston Cup championship, met with the media at the Robert Yates Racing shop in Charlotte. (Francisco Kjolseth/Charlotte Observer)

There's another important part of that lesson, too, a part that Jarrett learned from his father.

"No matter what goes on, it's how you treat people and the respect that you show them is what you are going to get in return," Dale Jarrett said. "My dad always told me as I started into the business that you treat people the way that you want to be treated. Regardless of what else may have happened and what goes on around you, you continue with that and good things are going to come out of it.

"You have to learn to deal with people and get along with people. Nobody has a job they can totally do by themselves. They have to rely on somebody else somewhere along the way. You have to learn to get along with people, and those who do that are the people who learn to succeed.

"It takes everybody to make it work. There is no one person on my team who can do all of the jobs and make this work. You simply can't do it. It's teamwork. Wherever people work, it has to run just like this team. You have to get along with the people you work with and work around and that's the only way you're going to be successful."

Ned Jarrett is proud that his son learned the lesson so well.

"How he persevered to get to where he is today, and also the type of person that he is and how he has handled things over the years. Those are the things we're proud of," Ned said. "The type of father and husband he is and the things he does in the community that a lot of people don't know about. "The kind of person he is, that's what we're proud of. How he does on the race track is a bonus as far as we're concerned."

In 1999, the bonus was as big one. Counting the check for nearly $3 million he collected in New York, Jarrett's team earned $6,649,596 on its way to NASCAR's title.

Remember that envelope Jarrett still has from his first race at Hickory in 1977? The one in which he got $35 for finishing ninth?

The money he won 22 years later would fill 189,988 of those.

Dale talks with reporters after practicing for qualification at Martinsville Speedway. (Todd Sumlin/ Charlotte Observer)

Dale Jarrett Quick Facts

Birthdate: November 26, 1956.
Birthplace: Newton, N.C.
Home: Hickory, N.C.
Family: Jarrett and his wife, Kelley, have three children—Natalee (born March 26, 1988), Karsyn (born April 11, 1990) and Zachary (born Dec. 8, 1994). Jarrett also has a son, Jason (born Oct. 14, 1975), from a previous marriage. Jason Jarrett is a racer who will drive the Grand National series car his father owns in the 2000 season.
Hobbies: Jarrett enjoys playing golf and spending time outdoors.
Other interests: Jarrett is one of the most active drivers in charity work. He was named NASCAR's Man of the Year in 1996 for his efforts to raise money for the Brenner Children's Hospital in Winston-Salem, N.C., and for Carly Brayton, whose father, Indy-car driver Scott Brayton, suffered fatal injuries in a wreck prior to the 1996 Indianapolis 500. In 1998 and 1999, Dale and Kelley Jarrett have worked on behalf of the Susan G. Komen Foundation for breast cancer research. The Jarretts, with the help of their race team sponsors, raised $220,000 for that charity in 1999 alone.
Race team: Robert Yates Racing.
Shop location: Charlotte, N.C.

Career Highlights

Career starts:
389.
First start:
April 29, 1984, at Martinsville. Jarrett started
24th, finished 14th.
First victory:
June 18, 1991, in Champion 400 at Michigan
Speedway, his 129th start.
Most recent victory:
Aug. 7, 1999 in Brickyard 400 at Indianapolis
Motor Speedway.
Poles:
7
First pole:
Feb. 11, 1995, for Daytona 500 in
his 230th career start.
Most recent pole:
Sept. 4, 1998 for Southern 500
at Darlington Raceway.

Career Victories

1991
Michigan (Aug. 18).

1993
Daytona 500 (Feb. 14).

1994
Charlotte (Oct. 9).

1995
Pocono (July 16)

1996
Daytona (Feb. 18), Charlotte (May 26), Indianapolis (Aug. 3), Michigan (Aug. 18)

1997
Atlanta (March 9), Darlington (March 23), Pocono (July 20), Bristol (Aug. 23), Richmond (Sept. 6), Charlotte (Oct. 5), Phoenix (Nov. 2).

1998
Darlington (March 22), Charlotte (May 31), Talladega (Oct. 11)

1999
Richmond (May 15), Michigan (June 13),

Career record

Starts	Starts	Poles	Wins	Top 5s	Top 10s	DNFs	Races Led	Laps Led	Money Won
Super Speedways	265	7	19	87	121	62	113	4,516	6,974,012
Short Tracks	97	0	3	23	40	19	21	1,138	------
Road Courses	27	0	0	4	6	6	5	26	------
Career	389	7	22	114	167	87	139	5,680	21,962,615
1999 Season	34	0	4	24	29	1	22	1,061	6,649,596

NASCAR's All-Time Money Winners

DRIVER	CAREER STARTS	WINNINGS	AVERAGE PER START
1. Dale Earnhardt	641	$36,526,665	$56,983
2. Jeff Gordon	223	$31,867,679	$142,904
3. Mark Martin	424	$22,269,442	$52,522
4. Dale Jarrett	389	$21,962,615	$56,459
5. Terry Labonte	641	$21,285,075	$33,206
6. Rusty Wallace	492	$21,247,599	$43,186
7. Bill Elliott	591	$21,107,334	$35,715
8. Darrell Waltrip	780	$18,170,338	$23,295
9. Ricky Rudd	661	$16,737,226	$25,231
10. Geoffrey Bodine	538	$14,044,433	$26,104

Dale Jarrett's Ride

Team:
Robert Yates Racing
Owner:
Robert Yates
Car number:
88.
Make:
Ford Taurus
Sponsors:
Ford Credit and Ford Quality Care
Colors:
Blue, red and white
Crew chief:
Todd Parrott
Fuel system:
22 gallons
Tires:
Goodyear Racing Eagles
Weight:
3,400 pounds
Horsepower:
700@8000 rpm

Baseball Superstar Series Titles
Collect Them All!

___ Mark McGwire: Mac Attack!

___ #1 *Derek Jeter: The Yankee Kid*

___ #2 *Ken Griffey Jr.: The Home Run Kid*

___ #3 *Randy Johnson: Arizona Heat!*

___ #4 *Sammy Sosa: Slammin' Sammy*

___ #5 *Bernie Williams: Quiet Superstar*

___ #6 *Omar Vizquel: The Man with the Golden Glove*

___ #7 *Mo Vaughn: Angel on a Mission*

___ #8 *Pedro Martinez: Throwing Strikes*

___ #9 *Juan Gonzalez: Juan Gone!*

___ #10 *Tony Gwynn: Mr. Padre*

___ #11 *Kevin Brown: Kevin with a "K"*

___ #12 *Mike Piazza: Mike and the Mets*

___ #13 *Larry Walker: Canadian Rocky*

___ #14 *Nomar Garciaparra: High 5!*

___ #15 *Sandy and Roberto Alomar: Baseball Brothers*

___ #16 *Mark Grace: Winning with Grace*

___ #17 *Curt Schilling: Phillie Phire!*

___ #18 *Alex Rodriguez: A+ Shortstop*

___ #19 *Roger Clemens: Rocket!*

Only $4.95 per book!

Call Toll Free: 1-877-424-BOOK (2665) or visit us at www.sportspublishinginc.com

Basketball Superstar Series Titles
Collect Them All!

___ #1 *Kobe Bryant: The Hollywood Kid*

___ #2 *Keith Van Horn: Nothing But Net*

___ #3 *Antoine Walker: Kentucky Celtic*

___ #4 *Kevin Garnett: Scratching the Surface*

___ #5 *Tim Duncan: Slam Duncan*

___ #6 *Reggie Miller: From Downtown*

___ #7 *Jason Kidd: Rising Sun*

___ #8 *Vince Carter: Air Canada*

Only $4.95 per book!

NASCAR Superstar Series Titles

___ #1 *Jeff Gordon: Rewriting the Record Books*

___ #2 *Dale Jarrett: Son of Thunder*

___ #3 *Dale Earnhardt: The Intimidator*

___ #4 *Tony Stewart: Hottest Thing on Wheels*

Hockey Superstar Series Titles

___ #1 *John LeClair: Flying High*

___ #2 *Mike Richter: Gotham Goalie*

___ #3 *Paul Kariya: Maine Man*

___ #4 *Dominik Hasek: The Dominator*

___ #5 *Jaromir Jagr: Czechmate*

___ #6 *Martin Brodeur: Picture Perfect*

___ #8 *Ray Bourque: Bruins Legend*

Only $4.95 per book!

Collect Them All!